REAL ESTATE INVESTING: HOW TO GET RICH & BE A SMART REAL ESTATE INVESTOR

Learn How To: Buy & Hold Residential Properties, Manage Rental Properties, Negotiate Deals, & Create Passive Income Forever

A Power Pack Success Production

By Nigel Francis

About The Author

"So you think, so shall you become"

- Bruce Lee

"Many people in life are frozen, frustrated, and struggling with many vices and problems that are holding them back from achieving the prosperous and abundant lives that they deserve to live. The truth is, everyone deserves to be great in life, and moreover, everyone is capable of doing so. Each and every single individual on this planet has a glorious purpose rooted deep within their being and I feel that it is my purpose, as a Christian first, to help others to access that purpose and to reach their full blown potential. Helping others gives me satisfaction, helping others will help me to sleep well at night. If I can make an impact and influence one person in my life to make a positive and impactful change in themselves, I know that I have done my job. I want to help people, that is what I want to do. I want to strive to be that change in the world that people want to see, and in doing so, I want to influence others to be that change as well."

- Nigel

Nigel is an online entrepreneur, publisher, and motivational speaker that seeks to help people in various areas of their lives because he at one time struggled with depression, addiction, and and financial struggles. While many people create content merely

merely just to make a dollar, Nigel has made a lifetime commitment to empowering and helping others around the world. In fact, Nigel left his career in finance, a former dream of of his, because he wanted to pursue something that was more fulfilling to him that would truly change and impact other people people worldwide. His desire to help others is conveyed in the books that he publishes in which he simply aims to help people overcome their problems in order to enhance their day to day lives. He truly takes pride in his services and in providing high quality content to his peers.

In his spare time, Nigel goes to church with his wife, travels, works out, reads books, watches movies, and likes to spend time and go on adventures with his friends and family.

Lastly, and most importantly, he is an avid sports fan and loves his teams: The New York Knicks and New York Giants.

Table of Contents

Introduction 1

PART ONE: THE FUNDAMENTALS OF REAL ESTATE INVESTING 4

Chapter One: What's so Special About Real Estate? 5

Chapter Two: Am I Cut Out For Real Estate Investing? 11

Chapter Three: Property Investing Strategies 15

Chapter Four: Types of Rental Properties 22

Chapter Five: Finding the Right Investment Property 30

PART TWO: COLLABORATIONS AND FINANCING 38

Chapter Six: The Real Estate Agent 39

Chapter Seven: The Other Key Team Members 43

Chapter Eight: Preparing and Submitting an Offer 50

Chapter Nine: Getting Financing for the Deal 55

Chapter Ten: Closing a Real Estate Deal 62

PART THREE: MANAGING YOUR PROPERTY 66

Chapter Eleven: Rental Property Management........................67

Chapter Twelve: How to Deal with Troublesome Tenants 72

Conclusion 75

Resources...79

Introduction

Real estate has always been one of the most popular ways to make money and generate sustainable wealth. A lot of people are aware of this fact, which is why you will find numerous books being sold on how to get through rich investing in real estate.

However, one thing is for certain. Most budding real estate investors are not really achieving the success they anticipated. There seems to be a surplus of real estate investing information but not enough genuine and effective guidance on how you can acquire the right knowledge and then use it to get rich. On top of that, most of the information out there is so outdated that the strategies won't even work in today's market economy. This is the problem that most real estate investors face today, especially those who are just starting out.

This is where this book separates itself from the pack. In this book, *"Real Estate Investing: How to Get Rich & Be a Smart Real Estate Investor,"* you will find some of the most current and best advice on real estate investing. The answers to the questions that have been plaguing you will be found right here, so be prepared to learn some critical information that very few industry insiders will ever reveal.

This book is based on the 10+ years of experience and research that I have carried out as a property manager, real estate agent, and now as an investor myself. Throughout this time, I have seen

seen people achieve phenomenal success, but I have also seen many others lose everything they had. I kid you not, most online online resources will paint a rosy picture of real estate investing, investing, but if you don't have a clue about what you are doing, doing, you will be eaten alive. These are shark-infested waters, and my job from now on until you finish this book is to guide you you on where to go and how to maneuver your way to success. Real estate is very lucrative, and I want you to enjoy the experience and get rich doing it.

So what can you expect to gain from this book?

The book is structured in three parts. In the first part of the book, you will learn some of the motivations for investing in real estate. What's so special about real estate and is it the right type of investment for you? You will also learn about some of the best property investment strategies to use and the different types of properties to buy. One of the most crucial aspects of real estate investing is identifying the right property. I will show you step-by-step how to find exactly what you are looking for.

The second part of the book covers the collaboration and financial aspects of real estate. You will learn how to assemble a team of competent lawyers, accountants, contractors, and agents who will help you get your dream off the ground. I will also show you how to negotiate offers, obtain financing, and close real estate deals.

The final part of the book will cover some handy techniques that you can use to manage your properties effectively, including some tips on how to deal with bad tenants.

This is the kind of advice that people pay thousands of dollars for in seminars and conferences. You are getting it here wrapped up in this book.

I want you to get excited from the get-go about this adventure, so it's important that you know for sure that this is something you want to do. I can promise you that what you are about to learn will have a major impact on the wealth and success you achieve through real estate investing. All you need to do now is take action.

If you have been waiting for a book that encapsulates everything necessary to invest in real estate and finally achieve the passive income you've always wanted, this book is it.

Are you ready to become a smart and wealthy real estate investor?

Read on!

PART ONE:

THE FUNDAMENTALS OF REAL ESTATE INVESTING

Chapter One: What's so Special About Real Estate?

In this chapter, you will learn why investing in real estate is a great idea. There are numerous benefits to it, yet at the same time, I cannot hide the fact that there are some risks to watch out for. It is important that you begin on the right footing, so let's look at what your motivations may be and evaluate real estate as an investment vehicle.

The Potential of Real Estate

Why should you invest in real estate? Why not go for something like the stock market or maybe start a small business?

If you have already made up your mind to become an investor, you should ensure that you choose the right investment vehicle to help you achieve your goals. There are many options available, but not all investments are created equal.

Real estate has its own unique characteristics that make it much more lucrative than other forms of investments. At the same time, there are some aspects that aren't so positive.

Let's take a look at some of the unique characteristics that define define real estate so that you know whether it's worth your while:

while:

1. **Healthy returns** – Real estate has the ability to provide continuous income even as the value of the property appreciates. In essence, you can own an asset that produces an annual rate of return of about 10 percent, and this can increase if you identify the right property in the right location and manage it well.

2. **Low volatility** – Before you start thinking about the decline in real estate that occurred in 2008, please consider that compared to stock prices, real estate generally doesn't suffer as much. Though you may run the risk of losing anywhere between 10 to 30 percent of your investment during a market downturn, this usually happens to short-term investors who aren't willing to wait it out. This is why I advocate for the buy-and-hold strategy which you will learn more about later on in this book.

3. **Large capital investment** – Investing in the stock market these days is fairly easy if you have a few hundred dollars to spare. Everyone seems to be getting in on the action. Real estate, however, requires a much larger investment. This is especially true if you want to acquire high-quality properties.

4. **Value addition** – Once you buy stocks, you cannot add value to them. However, real estate is different because you can buy property on the cheap, refurbish it, and sell it for a lot more money. If it's a rental property, this may also allow you to increase the rent and earn greater income.

5. **Poor liquidity** – Liquidity can be defined as the ease of of selling an asset and recouping your investment. Real estate is not a very liquid asset. With stocks, all you have

to do is make an order to sell and the money hits your bank account. Selling real estate takes time, effort, and costs a lot of money in transaction fees. On the other hand, the *illiquidity* of real estate can actually be a good thing. It forces you to think long-term, and as a result, you you hold on to your investment until the time is right to offload it.

6. **Tax benefits** – With real estate, you get a tax deduction for depreciation of property. When you sell some property and use the profit to invest in another piece of real estate, you also avoid paying taxes on the money you received. There are also special tax credits for investors who buy and upgrade historic buildings and low-income residential properties.

These are just some of the major characteristics of real estate as an investment compared to other traditional investment vehicles. So now that you have got a taste of what makes real estate investing so special, let's move on to some of the specific benefits.

Benefits of Real Estate Investing
These are the major benefits of investing in real estate:

1. **A regular flow of cash** – When you invest in rental properties, you ensure that you receive regular income every month. Of course, you have to keep an eye out for expenses such as maintenance, mortgage payments, and insurance when calculating your monthly cash flow.

2. **Lower income tax payments** – You are allowed to reduce your income tax by claiming depreciation costs for your property. This will give your cash flow a boost.

3. **Tax-deferred compounding** – Apart from depreciation lowering your income tax, owning property also means you don't pay taxes even as the asset appreciates in value over the years. You will only be legally required to pay taxes when you finally sell your property and take a hold of the profits. As I described before, you can still avoid these taxes by simply investing in another property using the same profits.

4. **Rental income increases faster than overall expenses** – As time goes by, your operating profit will increase at a faster rate compared to any expenses you incur on the property.

5. **Access to greater credit** – The income that you generate from your real estate investments is proof to lending institutions that you are a viable candidate for more credit. It opens up more doors to access loans for other investments.

Drawbacks of Real Estate Investing

Though the benefits are many, real estate investing isn't profitable for everyone at all times. There are times when some drawbacks may arise. Here are some highlights:

1. **Getting financing** – Most lenders won't give you a loan loan to invest in real estate unless you are able to provide provide 20+ percent down payment. Then there are the

eligibility requirements that must be met. These can lock lock out some people altogether.

2. **Getting into debt** – Most investors have to use loans to finance their real estate acquisitions. If you buy some property with the intention of flipping it and no buyer comes along, you may get saddled with the debt until you are able to offload the asset. If you fail to manage your rental properties well and tenants default on rent, you may find yourself forced to go to the courts to evict the tenant. The cost of hiring a lawyer will simply add more debt to what you already owe your lender.

3. **Maintenance and repair costs** – As the owner of rental property, you are legally required to keep the building in good shape by executing regular repairs. Fixing the roof or HVAC of a large apartment complex is not cheap, and if you don't undertake repairs on time as required by the local authority, you can expect a hefty fine.

4. **Lawsuits for personal injury** – I'm sure you've heard the stories. Something falls on someone, they get hurt, and the owner of the property gets sued for damages. Or maybe someone slips and falls when walking on someone's property and the owner gets sued. As the owner of the real estate, you are legally liable to pay their medical fees, not to mention damages and lawyer fees.

5. **Exorbitant transaction costs** – One of the worst decisions you can make is to buy a property and then decide to get rid of it in less than two years. Though the value may have appreciated, the high transaction costs involved will totally eliminate any profits you make when

when you sell it. The process of buying and selling real estate is costly due to the agent commissions, title insurance, loan fees, closing costs, etc. These expenses can can go as high as 15 percent of the buying price of the asset. If you sell your property too quickly, all you will get get is a meager appreciation in value, and this too will be be wiped out by the high transaction costs.

You now have a somewhat clear idea of what you are getting yourself into. Real estate investing has its benefits as well as its drawbacks. Ultimately, my advice is that you go ahead and invest in real estate. Why? Because the best way to overcome any risks or drawbacks is to acquire the right knowledge! That's what this book will help you do.

In the next chapter, you will learn some of the factors that determine whether you are cut out for real estate success.

Chapter Two: Am I Cut Out For Real Estate Investing?

In this chapter, I intend to help you determine whether you have what it takes to hack it as a successful real estate investor. There are certain factors that help you know if you are ready for this kind of challenge. I am going to guide you through an in-depth analysis of your life so that you are able to make this decision on your own. I will ask a series of questions, and you should do your best to examine yourself and be as honest as possible. Not everyone can succeed at this kind of investing, so get ready to face a stern test!

Can You Commit your Personal Time?

What does your average work week look like? The truth of real estate investing is this: It is extremely time-consuming. Look at it this way. You have to take the time to find the right rental property and do your due diligence. If you don't, you will discover that the property you just bought has a host of problems that will cost you more time and money to fix.

Then you have to take the time to find a competent real estate agent, investigate the neighborhood, examine potential tenants, tenants, handle repairs, etc. Even if you decide to hire a manager manager to take care of the property, you will still need to devote devote some time to approve costs of repairs and communicate regularly with them.

Here's my advice to you. If you think that you cannot afford to spare some time out of your already busy schedule to handle these mundane issues, then investing in rentals isn't for you. There are other ways to invest in real estate that don't consume so much time, for example, REITs, notes, and tax liens. These are discussed in Chapter 3.

Are You a Problem-Solver?

Owning property can be very stressful. The process of negotiating a deal to buy property can be frustrating at times, and that's even before you start managing tenants and paying maintenance costs.

If you are the kind of person who doesn't like dealing with small issues raised by tenants or major repairs caused by unruly renters, you should probably get the help of a property manager. Even then, there will still be problems cropping up now and then. If you aren't the type who is ready to tackle all kinds of problems from day-to-day, then maybe owning rental property isn't for you.

Are You Passionate About Real Estate?

There are some people who simply love owning and managing real estate. They enjoy dealing with their real estate investment personally and are always curious about learning more. These are the kind of investors who thrive as property owners and managers.

This doesn't mean that you cannot develop this level of interest over time. You just need to buy some property and create that passion as you gain more experience. On the other hand, there are seasoned investors who may have made millions in the stock stock market but don't have the passion for real estate. They try try their hand and realize it's simply not for them. You need to decide whether you love owning and managing real estate or are are just forcing yourself into something which you have no genuine interest.

Are You Mentally Prepared For Market Downturns?

You need to be prepared to face market downturns, both on a mental and emotional level. It may look like fun when property prices and rents are going up, but when the market goes into a freefall, it's easy to lose your cool. There will always be ups and downs in the market, so you have to make the decision beforehand that you are willing to wait it out instead of engaging in panic selling. It helps if you have had some experience handling other kinds of investments during economic downturns.

Are You Already In Debt?

If you are already struggling to pay off your consumer debts, then I would advise you to stay away from investing in real estate - at least in the meantime. People who have terrible spending habits and waste their money on things that they don't need aren't cut out for this kind of investment. First, try to live within your means and generate a surplus before you start thinking about investing in something like real estate.

As you can see, investing in real estate requires you to sit down and think about some serious aspects of your life. There is no point in rushing into something that you clearly are not prepared for. The factors that we have discussed in this chapter will determine whether you are able to succeed as a real estate investor or not. Don't take them lightly. Think about what we have discussed here and then make a decision. If you are ready to move into real estate investing, then do it.

In the next chapter, you will learn some of the real estate investing strategies that are guaranteed to help you get rich as a property investor.

Chapter Three: Property Investing Strategies

In this chapter, you will learn three of the biggest strategies for investing in real estate. So far we have not yet talked about the different niches that you can use when investing in rental property, but before we move into that, I want you to get a hold of this knowledge of how to invest wisely to generate wealth.

So what are these three common techniques used in real estate investing?

Buy-and-Hold Strategy

This is considered to be one of the most common investment strategies in real estate. Buy-and-hold simply means that you purchase a piece of property, rent it out for a couple of years, and use it to accumulate wealth. It is a very simple form of investing that anyone can adopt.

If you intend to use this strategy, you will be able to collect monthly rent from tenants and use this income to reduce the mortgage on the building. This is an awesome way to minimize your loan balance while boosting your equity portfolio. Alternatively, you can also decide to hold on to the asset, keep it in good condition, and then sell it for a huge profit somewhere down the line.

If you are just starting out as a real estate investor, one of the biggest pieces of advice I can give you is this: learn how to assess every real estate deal or opportunity you come across. I have seen many new investors make terrible mistakes when using the buy-and-hold strategy. If you haven't figured out how to properly evaluate real estate, you are likely to get a bad deal.

There are also many other problems that you need to watch out for, including underestimating the expenses that come with the property, choosing the wrong type of tenants, and not managing the property properly. All these are problems that you can resolve right now by getting the right education. Instead of jumping in head first, you need to learn how the business works, which is what I want to teach you in this book. It may not seem like it at first, but there are potentially many financial and legal implications of making unwise choices using buy-and-hold.

So what exactly is the right way to implement this investing strategy?

One of the first things you have to do is examine the location of the property and the market around it. Learn to identify how the market peaks and declines, that is, the cycle that the local property market goes through. Every real estate market follows a similar cycle as follows:

- **Peak** – This is where property prices are at their highest and there is very little real estate available for purchase.

- **Tipping point** – This is where prices start to go down and foreclosures start to increase.

- **Decline** – As prices keep falling, homeowners lose their homes due to inability to pay debts. Most people avoid buying property, thus causing an increase in available real estate at cheap prices.

- **Bottom** – Prices hit rock bottom, homeowners are eager to sell their property, and real estate investors flood the market, grabbing as much property as they can.

- **Climb** – As prices begin to rise again, homeowners gain more confidence and fewer houses are sold.

A smart buy-and-hold investor will always wait until the market declines and property prices fall before they snap up any real estate. The moment that the market rebounds and prices start peaking, you should stop buying and wait for things to cool down. During these periods, you can settle down and collect rental income, or even decide to sell the property at a profit. However, as I advised earlier, it's always good to hold on to the asset for a couple of years to avoid the hefty transaction costs eating up your profits.

As long as you are able to learn how to assess the market and find good deals, pick the right kind of tenants, and learn how to manage your property well, the buy-and-hold strategy will help you achieve success in real estate investing. It's all about reading the market cycle and timing the drop in prices.

House Flipping Strategy

This is a strategy that has been highlighted in numerous TV shows, which is why everyone rushes to use this technique. House flipping involves purchasing real estate at cheap prices, refurbishing it where necessary, and then offloading it for a huge huge profit. The main feature of house flipping is buying low and and selling high as *quickly* as possible. Speed is the key.

So how does this work?

Here is a good example. You identify a house that is valued at $100, 000. The rule of thumb for house flipping is that you purchase at 70 percent of the value and deduct the cost of refurbishment. So if repair costs will take about $15, 000, this house should cost you $55, 000 [($100, 000 x 0.7) - $15, 000]. After you fix up the house, you then sell it for the full amount of $100, 000.

Since the longer you hold on to the house the more expenses, taxes, and repairs you may have to encounter, it is in your best interest to find a buyer quickly. The house flipping strategy is very intensive because you have to keep looking for new real estate to buy, repair, and sell. Once you are done with one property, you must move on to the next one, and this makes this strategy more of an active income strategy than a passive one. But is it a viable and lucrative option? You bet!

Wholesaling Strategy

Wholesaling is a strategy that involves identifying a good piece of property, getting a contract to purchase the property, and then selling that contract to another investor. In other words, as a wholesaler, your job is to act as a middleman and sell real estate contracts for a fee. This is usually referred to as an "assignment fee" and can be anywhere from $500 to $5,000, depending on the size of the property.

If you use this wholesaling strategy, your primary buyers will be house flippers, though sometimes you can also sell the contract to a retail buyer. The great thing about dealing with house flippers is that they are also investors who want to make a quick deal, so they usually pay you in cash. This means that the wholesaling strategy can help you generate some solid cash within a few weeks or even days. This strategy also puts you in a position where you will interact with many other investors during the course of your work, thus expanding your network in the real

It is important to note that a wholesaler never really owns the property. This is one of the reasons why most new investors decide to adopt this strategy. It is simple and doesn't require a lot of capital to start. You won't have to deal with any banks, loan fees, tenants, contractors, or any other complex expenses. If you move around real estate investing circles, you will realize that most of the investment gurus teach this strategy to their students, and this has led to its popularity.

On the other hand, you shouldn't be fooled into thinking that it's just a bed of roses. You still have to do a lot of work to succeed as a real estate wholesaler. You have to constantly be on the lookout for great deals that will attract buyers. Getting buyers is also hard work, especially in the beginning.

Though some people claim that you can become a wholesaler with absolutely no money at all, you still need some cash to invest in creating a marketing funnel. Remember that you are a middleman acquiring and selling contracts, so the most important thing is to market yourself as someone who has access to the best deals. Otherwise, you may find yourself stuck with a bunch of contracts with no buyers forthcoming and no money to pay for the properties yourself!

REITs, Tax Liens, and Notes

In this section, I want to talk about some of the ways of investing in real estate without necessarily buying rental properties. These are strategies that you can use but are also considered to be niches of real estate investing.

1. **REITs** – Real Estate Investment Trusts are like mutual funds in the stock market. A group of investors come together, pool their money to create a REIT, and then use the funds to invest in large real estate projects like apartment complexes, shopping malls, or an entire neighborhood of residential homes. It is a very passive approach. To get involved, purchase some REIT shares in the stock market and wait to receive your dividends.

2. **Tax liens** – Whenever a homeowner fails to meet their tax obligations, the government can repossess their house and sell it to investors to recover the money owed. This can provide you with an opportunity to acquire real estate at a heavily discounted price, though I would advise you to assess the deal properly first. Tax liens are complex transactions that need extensive research and experience.

3. **Notes** – This is where you buy a paper mortgage from a property owner. Let's say that someone who owns an apartment complex decides to sell the asset to a buyer for for $10 million. Under normal circumstances, the buyer would be forced to get a bank loan to pay for the apartment complex. However, the owner decides to create create a contract or "note" where instead of the buyer getting a bank loan, they agree to pay the owner 10 percent every year until the whole amount is paid off. If

after a while the owner decides he wants to get out of the
the deal, he simply sells the "note" to an investor. If you
buy the note, you give the owner an agreed sum (usually
less than he would have made had he kept the contract)
and start receiving the yearly payments. You can also
decide to sell the note later on if you wish.

You have now learned some of the key strategies that you can use
in real estate investing to generate wealth. If you still aren't
certain which one is right for you, it's OK. We are just getting
started. Becoming a smart real estate investor takes time, and as
you continue reading this book, you will begin to enhance your
understanding of what to do to succeed as an investor.

In the next chapter, you will learn about some of the different
types of properties that you can invest in.

Chapter Four: Types of Rental Properties

In this chapter, we will cover the various types of rental properties that you can invest in to start receiving passive income. We will be looking at single-family homes, multifamily properties, small commercial apartments, commercial real estate, and mobile homes.

Single-Family Homes

This is, without doubt, the most common type of rental investment for investors who are dabbling in real estate for the first time. Single-family rentals (SFRs) can be easily financed, easily rented out, and are easy to sell. However, the one negative thing that I can point out is that in most locations, rent from SFRs will not be high enough to generate a positive cash flow.

So how do you go about investing in SFRs? Here are some tips:

1. **Expand your search area** – You need to do some research to identify the right property, even if it means going outside your local area or state. Some markets will have SFRs going for as much as hundreds of thousands of of dollars, but if you keep looking, you will find that there there are places where you can get real estate for as little as $50,000. If your local area isn't conducive to your pocket, don't be afraid to expand your search to new

markets. Use the internet to get listings and view some images, and then drive down to the area to scan the neighborhood. Companies like *www.roofstock.com* provide a list of homes that they have already leased and the expected returns you get when you buy. Then there is is *www.auction.com* that gives you a database of SFRs that have been foreclosed nationwide.

2. **Find a good property manager** – Once you have bought a single-family rental, you need to make sure that you make your investment as profitable as possible. If the property is in your local area, you can manage it yourself. However, if it is far away and you plan on growing your real estate investments, you should consider working with a property management company. A good place to find both SFRs and good managers is *www.renterswarehouse.com*.

Multifamily Properties

Many real estate investors buy into the myth that bigger is better, and they consequently ignore rental properties like duplexes, triplexes, and quads and look for larger commercial properties. However, multifamily properties can be very profitable investments. They are available in many different locations, generate greater returns, and can be bought at better terms compared to larger real estate assets.

But what exactly are multifamily properties?

These are buildings that can house anywhere from two to four units. If you are interested in buying property that has two to four four units, you can easily do so as an individual. However, if the the property is much larger, it may be a good idea to pool funds with others and invest together. This may help to minimize the burden of vacancy expenses, debt servicing, and management costs.

Some of the advantages of investing in multifamily properties include:

1. Less competition since they mostly attract individual buyers rather than investment groups/institutions.

2. They generate greater cash flow. The internal rates of return and cash-on-cash returns are very high.

3. You don't require a lot of equity to buy multifamily properties. You can take one loan to buy some or all the units in the building. In fact, banks view multifamily homes that have four units or less the same way as single-family homes.

4. They can provide you with a home to live in even as you manage the other units in the property.

5. The sellers of multifamily properties are generally very flexible and thus the deal can be closed much faster compared to larger properties.

Commercial Apartments

If you have been dealing with SFRs and multifamily units for a while, you can decide that it's time to branch into commercial apartments. These are properties that contain five or more units, units, and financing them is usually much more difficult than smaller properties. This is because the lenders view these properties from a commercial rather than residential perspective. perspective. This doesn't mean that they aren't used for residential purposes. It is simply a way of separating them from from the smaller types of rental properties.

Commercial apartments generate a lot of positive cash flow, even though you must be ready to commit yourself to becoming a more involved manager/owner. There is generally very little competition for such properties because group investors such as REITs perceive them to be small while newbie investors see them as too large.

Their value is based on how much rental income they generate. This means that if you buy such properties, you can easily add value by increasing rents, minimizing expenses, and managing it effectively. It would be a good idea to hire a manager who lives in the building and performs regular maintenance. Instead of paying them a salary, you can offer the manager free or reduced rent.

So how do you go about finding commercial apartments for sale?

Well, you could check out the MLS (multiple listing services), but you will quickly discover that there are very few apartments on sale there. This is because commercial listings are rarely placed on the MLS.

The other alternative is to reach out to a commercial real estate investment broker. These brokers are in constant contact with property owners and are always aware of any sale opportunities. opportunities. Brokers tend to have a list of potential investors lined up just in case something becomes available. All you need to to do is connect to different commercial brokers who focus on the the same areas as you. Get to know them, tell them how much you are willing to invest, and they will put you on their list. Make Make sure you stay in constant communication so that when a

property is on sale, they will quickly remember you and connect
connect you with the owner.

Commercial Real Estate

This is a property that is for commercial use and not residential
purposes. They are normally leased to businesses and come in
various sizes, styles, and uses. For example, you can decide to
invest in small buildings that house small stores or you can
purchase and rent out large spaces to megastores and large
supermarkets.

The good thing about commercial real estate is that they will
generate great cash flow and rental income will be consistent. On
the other hand, when a business moves out, space may remain
unoccupied for a very long time. It's not uncommon to see a
commercial property with space that has been empty for years.

Just to be clear, commercial real estate is not an option that
beginners should consider unless you have a huge amount of cash
to splash and are willing to dive into the deep end from the get-
go.

Even then, I would advise you to get to understand the basics first
and educate yourself on how to run a commercial property. Most
new investors assume that all they have to do is enter some
numbers into a spreadsheet and use formulas to get all the
information they need. However, will you even be aware of what
the information you are looking at means for your bottom line?

Here are some things to consider when investing in commercial
real estate:

1. **Learn the lingo** – Make sure that you understand concepts such as operating expenses, gross income, effective gross income (EGI), net operating income (NOI), vacancy rate, debt service, cap rate, and cash-on-cash return.

2. **Understand the corresponding percentages** – Once you understand what the terms and concepts above mean, you also need to find out the acceptable percentages for each of them. What is regarded as a high vacancy rate? How much of gross income do operating expenses consume? You need to know how to calculate these things quickly so that you are able to negotiate a good deal.

3. **Learn how to interpret the numbers** – So now that you know all the terminologies and understand the percentages, you still need to interpret the numbers. Do you know the difference between a 5 percent cap rate in your local market versus a 10 percent cap rate in another market? What about 55 percent operating expenses on a property versus 30 percent operating expenses on a similar type of property? It is important that you understand the picture that the numbers are painting.

Mobile Homes

There is a growing demand for cheap housing, and mobile homes homes are definitely a viable investment strategy. They generally generally provide affordable housing for those people who don't don't earn much money and are living just under the poverty level. Of course, this type of tenant is likely to put off some real estate investors, but for a smart investor, mobile homes present a present a great opportunity to make some money. The important important thing is to do your due diligence before buying anything.

Mobile homes have some amazing advantages, including:

1. A higher capitalization rate compared to all other types of real estate.

2. The demand for mobile homes continues to rise, thus driving up the value of mobile parks.

3. The owners tend to be the original investors. It is highly unlikely that you will require a loan to buy a mobile home from them since carry the financing.

4. The owners are usually reluctant to move the home somewhere else when they are relocating, so they would rather sell it to an investor.

Mobile homes are a good option, just as long as you watch out for certain criteria, such as the age of the house, its location, access to utilities, the income rate of potential tenants in the area, and local regulations.

The above types of properties are great options to help you get started in your real estate investing career. Obviously, some are a better fit for you than others. The best advice I can give you is to pick one or two of the above niches and focus on making money through them. Do your best to learn everything about them and become a pro at investing in that specific type of real estate. Once you have done that, you can go ahead and try your hand at some of the more complex types of properties.

In the next chapter, you are going to learn how to find the right properties that will maximize your wealth creation potential.

Chapter Five: Finding the Right Investment Property

In this chapter, you will learn how to find the best rental properties and negotiate deals that will leave you with a smile on your face. You will also learn where prime real estate investments can be made and how the buying process normally goes.

So far we have been focusing on learning how to prepare to enter the real estate market. However, sooner or later you will have to stop all the analyzing and just go out and purchase your first property. By the time you are through with this chapter, you should be able to do just that.

Be a Smart Buyer

In real estate, we have a saying that goes, "Your profit is made when you buy." In other words, whether you make a profit or not from a real estate deal is determined at the time of purchasing a property, not when selling it.

If you are a new investor, don't expect to begin your career by earning a large amount of money. You will only start reaping the the large monetary rewards once you have started to apply your your investment strategies. On the other hand, whether you make make a profit or a loss will be decided the moment you purchase purchase a property.

Let me put it this way. In order for you to make a profit when buying a property, you have to buy the property at a price that will give you a chance to make your desired profit, even as you contemplate your exit strategy. This simply means that you have to be a smart buyer. If you pay more money than necessary for a property, it won't matter how much you improve the property, hoping to make a profit off it later on. The market may decline and stay that way for a long time, and you may end up being forced to sell at sub-market prices.

The lesson here is that the only certainty you have is where the market is today. You don't know, and you can never predict with 100 percent certainty, what will happen in the market in the future.

For example, let's say that you find a rental property in an area where the average rent is $500 per month. Let's also say that the monthly expenses for the property add up to $700 per month. Is this a good deal? No! You will be losing money the moment you buy the property, regardless of how much you spruce up the place. On the other hand, if the average rents in the area are $1400 and the expenses are $700 a month, then you will be making a profit the moment you buy the property. That's what we mean when we say your profit is made when you buy.

Going Shopping For Property
Once you have understood the importance of locking in your profits at the buying phase of the deal, the next step is to begin searching for property. One of the first things you need to do is to come up with a list of criteria that will guide your search.

But why is it important to define your criteria early on?

Let's say that you're feeling inspired to cook a great fried chicken dinner for your friends. You go online to look for a great chicken recipe and find something that looks easy enough to make. You grab a pen, jot down the ingredients, and head for the store. In the store, you start picking out what you need, which will obviously be chicken, cooking oil, some herbs and spices, and etc.

However, you suddenly get a glimpse of some sweet potatoes and you remember a great sweet potato pie recipe that you've always wanted to try out. As you grab the sweet potatoes, it dawns on you that they aren't part of the ingredients on your list. They are merely a distraction, so you leave them behind and head home with exactly what you need for the chicken dinner.

This is what happens when investors go shopping for real estate. You will encounter many different properties that will entice you, and some of them will seem to be really sweet deals. If you don't have a predefined list of exactly what you are looking for in a property, you are likely to waste money on something that was merely a distraction. Worse still, you may suffer from "analysis paralysis," where you have so many options that you don't end up making a decision at all!

Having a list of criteria helps you to focus on what you really need so that you end up being pleased with what you end up with. You will be able to eliminate all other distractions quickly and only make deals that fit your investment interests.

Choosing Your Criteria

In the previous chapters, we looked at some of the types of rental rental properties you could invest in and the various strategies you can use. Now let's look at how to come up with a list of things things that will help you define your search for good investment investment property. Here are some of the key factors to consider:

- Neighborhood

- Town

- Size of the lot

- Size of the property in square feet

- Appreciation potential

- Cash flow

- Condition of the property

- Cap rate

- Number of units

I need to clarify right now that nobody can make the decision of what your criteria should be except you. Your criteria will reflect your personal preferences, for example, whether you want to buy property in Washington only or whether you are only interested in buildings with more than 10 units. However, the majority of your criteria will be based on your preferred type and strategy of investment. For example, if you want to buy property and hold on to it for a long time, then you should be looking for small and new properties instead of old buildings.

Another thing I want to mention is that having selection criteria criteria helps you to communicate your needs better to others.

When you tell people you are looking for property to buy, they may not be able to assist you, but when you tell them you are looking for a multifamily property in neighborhood X for less than $200,000, someone can easily give you ideas based on something they have seen or heard about.

Rules for Identifying the Right Property

The most critical aspect of your criteria list is money. A deal must be financially viable for you before you decide to invest. The problem is that you cannot figure out all the necessary financials of a particular property by simply looking at a listing in the newspaper or on a website. On the other hand, even if you acquired all the financial information you need, it wouldn't be possible to whip out your spreadsheet and fully evaluate every deal you come across. This is why you need to know the "rules" of property investing.

Rules help you to evaluate deals and make decisions quickly. Then again, don't rely upon them 100 percent because they are not very scientific. There are three rules I want to talk about here:

1. **The two percent rule** – According to this rule, you should charge monthly rent at two percent of the buying price of the property. If you purchase a home at $100,000, then you should charge a monthly rent of $2,000. Alternatively, if you find a home that rents for $1,000 a month, you should expect to spend at most $50,000 on it.

2. **The fifty percent rule** – According to this rule, 50 percent of your rental income will be consumed by expenses, excluding mortgage payments. For example, if you see a multifamily property listed as bringing in $10,000 a month as rental income, you should expect the expenses to be $5,000 per month. The remaining $5,000 is what you will use to pay the mortgage. If the mortgage payments amount to $4,000 a month, then your cash flow per month will be $1,000.

3. **The seventy percent rule** – This is usually used by house-flipping investors. In order to determine the purchase price of a house, you should take the selling price, multiply by 70 percent, and then subtract repair costs. If a property is being sold for $300,000 and requires $40,000 worth of repairs, then you should offer the seller (0.7 x $300,000) - $40,000, which is $170,000.

The above rules should not replace good old solid research. Use them to quickly decide whether a deal is good or a waste of money. If it passes the rules, go deeper and evaluate the property using a spreadsheet. Don't use these rules as an excuse to become a lazy investor.

How to Find Properties

Of course, you can drive around searching for "For Sale" signs in various neighborhoods, but there are other effective ways as well. Here are some ideas:

- **The Multiple Listing Service** – This is a list of available properties compiled by several real estate brokers all over the country. A site like www.realtor.com is is a good example.

- **Loopnet.com** – This happens to be the biggest online marketplace for real estate. Whatever type of property you are looking for, this website has it.

- **Craigslist** – This is a website that has a selection of items that people trade in, including properties.

- **Newspapers** – They have a limited range and selection of available properties, but they are still a good option.

- **Word of mouth** – This is how things were done back in the day, but surprisingly, some of the best deals can be found by word of mouth.

The Process of Buying Property

In this section, I would like to recap and provide a summary of what the buying process entails. Some of the steps have been covered already while others will be discussed in the next part of the book.

Here are the steps from start to finish:

1. Choose your investment strategy and type of property you want.

2. Create your list of criteria.

3. Choose how you will finance the deal e.g. loan, cash, etc.

4. Search the MLS, websites, classifieds, etc.

5. Filter each property you find through your criteria list and the three rules we talked about.

6. Make an offer, but always have a lawyer review the agreement documents first.

7. Negotiate with the property seller.

8. Inspect the property and hand over details to an attorney or an Escrow company. Verify and send in financing paperwork.

9. Sign the paperwork in the presence of an attorney or at the Escrow company.

We have now come to the end of Part one of the book. You have learned everything you need to know to have a firm foundation as a real estate investor. The information you have acquired in this chapter is very important, so make sure you go through it again.

In the next section of the book, we will be looking at how to assemble the right team as well as how to go about handling the the financing of property investments.

PART TWO:

COLLABORATIONS AND FINANCING

Chapter Six: The Real Estate Agent

In this chapter, you will learn how to work with a real estate agent and the value of collaborating with one. You will also learn some of the defining characteristics of a good real estate agent so that you know what to look out for.

Working with a Real Estate Agent

A real estate agent is one of the most important members of your real estate team. Since you are looking to generate passive income, you need to have professionals who can do the work on your behalf. A real estate agent has the expertise to help you find those really good deals that very few investors know about.

In most cities, it isn't enough to simply look for properties via the MLS, online listings, or in newspapers. Most of the best deals aren't advertised, so you are going to need an inside source to let you know when a lucrative offer becomes available. You want to be the first investor who is contacted rather than just another real estate buyer who saw a listing in the MLS.

As you consider working with an agent, you need to find out who they represent. You can either be dealing with a single agency or a dual agency. So what's the difference between the two?

A single agency is where the agent represents only one party – either the seller or the buyer of the property. In other words, each party has a different agent. Your agent will only promote your interests in the deal and keep all your personal information confidential. I would advise you to work with an agent who operates as a single agency. Income-generating property transactions involve huge sums of money so you need to work with someone who will look out for you alone.

A dual agency is where one real estate agent represents both seller and buyer of the property, or two agents from the same company represent the seller and the buyer respectively. The problem with this arrangement is that it makes it very difficult to maintain fiduciary loyalty to either party in the transaction. An agent may overhear the buyer saying that they are willing to offer more money, and then divulge this information to the seller. This conflict of interest has led some states in the US to either ban dual agency or force agents to inform their clients about the nature of their relationship.

Characteristics of a Good Agent

There are many real estate agents out there, but you need to have specific criteria that will help you weed out the undesirables and find those who are the best. Here are some characteristics you may need to consider:

1. **They must be a full-time professional** – There are many part-timers out there who are simply acting as real estate agents to get commissions. Choose an agent whom you know works full-time because these tend to be the most qualified.

2. **They know your market and property type** – Find an agent who is familiar with the geographical area of the market you are interested in. Agents also tend to specialize in specific property types, so don't hire someone who specializes in commercial apartments yet you are looking to buy a single-family home.

3. **They must have a current professional license** – Verify that the agent has a current real estate license and doesn't have any disciplinary cases, license suspensions, or pending violations. Check your state's online database of real estate agents.

4. **Confirm their references** – Ask the agent to give you the contacts of three clients they have represented in the last one year. Then call the clients and ask specific questions regarding the professionalism, experience, and work ethic of the agent.

5. **They must have good communication skills** – Most investors complain that real estate agents are not willing to communicate during transactions. It is important that you find someone who keeps you informed on a regular basis.

6. **They need to have interpersonal skills** – A good agent must be able to work with the other professionals in the transaction, namely lenders, sellers, and etc.

7. **They must be a good negotiator** – Negotiation is critical to a successful real estate deal, so your agent must be someone who does everything possible to give you the best deal.

8. **They must have a good reputation** – They need to be honest, patient and be of high integrity. Real estate deals can become testy at times, and only a real estate agent who is patient and trustworthy can save the day.

Real estate agents only get paid when the transaction goes through to the end, so it is in their best interests that the transaction is closed. It is therefore important that you work with an agent who will also put your interests first.

In the next chapter, you will learn about the other crucial members of your real estate investing team.

Chapter Seven: The Other Key Team Members

In this chapter, you will learn about some of the other professionals that you need to work with when investing in real estate. In the previous chapter, I highlighted the importance of a real estate agent and the role they play. Now you are going to learn why you also need an accountant, a contractor, and an attorney as part of your real estate investing team.

Hiring the Right Real Estate Accountant

Most real estate investors claim to have a hard time finding a good accountant. Yet an accountant is a very important component of every effective real estate team. Investing in real estate comes with some complexities, for example, tax preparation, business structuring, and deductions management. Are these things that you are competent in dealing with on a regular basis? I know I'm not, which is why we smart investors don't dare handle these issues on their own. They look for competent real estate accountants.

In case you are not convinced, here are some reasons why you need an accounting professional:

1. They will identify and leverage the numerous tax benefits that real estate investors are eligible for.

2. They are more competent to handle the tax code that seems to change all the time.

3. They will help you monitor your business transactions all year round.

4. They will create an organized financial record system for you. They will maintain financial records like leases, property sales, budgets, operational costs, cash-basis income statements, and everything else related to rental transactions

5. They can help you get in touch with the best attorneys, insurance agents, and real estate agents because they are aware of how these experts operate. They can even advise you on how to hire professionals while saving money.

Here's one thing I know. If you are doing all these things yourself, then you are most likely losing a lot of money OR working way too hard. A good accountant may seem to be expensive in the beginning, but in the long run, they will save you more money than you are paying them.

Interviewing an Accountant

One thing you must understand is that not all accountants are competent to the same level. In our case, we are interested in someone who knows what they are doing. When you have a few accountants to choose from, you are going to need some criteria to determine who is the most competent.

Here are some things to consider during the interview:

1. The kind of businesses they usually work with

2. The accounting niche do they specialize in

3. The number of clients they have who own income-generating real estate

4. Whether they work independently or are part of a firm

5. Whether they have other certifications apart from CPA

6. The services they can provide – Quickbooks, tax planning, tax returns, etc.

7. Years of accounting experience

8. Whether they too have invested in real estate

9. Cost of their services and whether they charge per year, per month, or hourly

10. Whether they know any techniques to help you save money on taxes

11. Any references that they can provide

Once you ask them questions related to the above, you should be in a good position to determine which accountant to work with.

Hiring an Attorney

Some investors seem to have this idea that an attorney is just an an expense and they will be fine without one. Well, if you are a beginner, you may be able to get by without an attorney since your first few deals will be small rentals. The forms are easy to fill fill and the real estate agent will walk you through them. In some some areas and states, attorneys are not required when closing real estate transactions, but some states have made it mandatory mandatory for attorneys to be involved.

I would suggest that you look for a professional real estate attorney when you start to engage in larger and more complex real estate transactions. You will realize that the paperwork is becoming more complex, and an attorney can help you review such documents. Though some escrow and title companies handle the paperwork for you, my advice is that you don't become dependent upon them. Get your own attorney, especially if you are using loans or looking for special financing.

Make sure that the attorney is a specialist in real estate lease and purchase transactions, tenant-landlord laws, commercial leases, and drafting of real estate documents. Ask other investors to refer you to a competent attorney who has good communication skills and can explain all the technical stuff in a simple way. Don't be tempted to go after a cheap attorney. When dealing with large property transactions, you want to be represented by someone with experience, even if they charge you an arm and a leg.

Hiring a Good Contractor

If you've ever had some work done in your house, then you know know that contractors are a dime a dozen, but a good contractor contractor is very hard to find. If you are flipping houses, getting getting a good contractor and building a long-term relationship with them should be your number one priority. They should be able to finish the job on time and within your budget, otherwise, otherwise, you will find it very difficult to make any profits. Sure, Sure, you may decide to fix the building on your own, but what if if you have multiple properties that need to be worked on?

Here are five reasons why you need a good contractor:

1. **It will free up your time** – As an investor, your main job should be to look for investments, not spend time running around buying supplies to fix up properties. You cannot be in different places at once, so why don't you focus on what the critical stuff and hire out the mundane tasks?

2. **You will become a better manager** – Through the process of hiring a contractor, you will gradually become better at managing a team. You will learn how to schedule work, supervise people, inspect work sites, and evaluate progress. These are invaluable skills.

3. **Your business will grow** – Delegating certain tasks means work is accomplished faster. You get to utilize your energy on growing the business while the contractor fixes the property efficiently.

4. **You become better at networking** – As you interview different contractors on a regular basis, you will learn how to network with people in the real estate industry. Sometimes you will be forced to ask for referrals or cold call people when you need help.

5. **It teaches you problem-solving skills** – There are times when things won't work out and a project will go off course, or a contractor will fail to deliver. You will have to fire people, rehire the work, and find ways to resolve problematic situations. Working with a contractor can teach you how to stay alert and handle problems when they come up.

Tips for Finding and Hiring a Contractor

Here are some tips to keep in mind when working with a contractor:

1. **Be slow to hire but quick to fire** – Be patient when looking for the right contractor. Don't just go online and hire a big company to refurbish a property. They will charge you triple the regular rate. Also, don't waste time when you find out that your contractor comes to work drunk in the morning or is running a sloppy operation. Get rid of them or they will cost you more money.

2. **Ask other investors for referrals** - You can contact other investors and ask their advice about good contractors they have worked with.

3. **Drive around the local area** - Drive around the area and when you see a house being repaired, stop and talk to the workers. Look at whether they talk respectfully, are sloppy in their work, or are meticulous in their work. Then ask for the contractor's business card.

4. **Write down the scope of work** – Keep this handy because you will need to refer to it many times.

5. **Put everything in writing** – Make sure that all the contracts and agreements are in place before the contractor starts work. Set a schedule of how work will be done and the contractor paid.

You now have a clear idea of what it takes to assemble a competent team of professionals to help you launch and grow your real estate investing business. An accountant, attorney, and and contractor are critical components of your vision to buy and

and hold property, generate passive income, and become wealthy. wealthy. Find the right people and you will succeed.

In the next chapter, we will talk about how to negotiate real estate offers.

Chapter Eight: Preparing and Submitting an Offer

In this chapter, you will learn how to negotiate and submit an offer to purchase real estate from the seller. We will talk about how to negotiate a deal that fits both you and the seller's needs.

How to Negotiate a Deal

Being a smart negotiator is one of the most important things when buying investment property. If you are able to negotiate a good deal for a property that is well-located and in good shape for a great price, you are guaranteed to receive excellent returns in the long run. In other words, if you want to continue to make passive income for a long time, you must learn how to combine great negotiating skills with great knowledge.

The right approach to negotiating is to understand that the real estate community is a tight-knit group. People talk to each other regularly, so one bad mention about your negotiating tactics may ruin your business long-term. There are two approaches that I would recommend you don't adopt.

The first one is the take-it-or-leave-it approach. Don't bulldoze the seller simply because the market is weak at the time of negotiating. If you want to stay active within that geographical location for a long time to come, you will need a good reputation.

reputation.

The second approach is low-balling. Don't make low offers to sellers as a tactic to get properties on the cheap. Sellers will quickly figure out that you are not a serious buyer, and when word spreads, you may be locked out of that market.

Get the Right Knowledge

Possessing superior information during a negotiation gives you the upper hand. This is why you need to spend time researching so that you don't pay more than the property is worth. You need to have knowledge of the properties in the neighborhood, state and local laws, and other economic data. If you don't have this knowledge, a stubborn seller will easily convince you to buy their property at a price higher than market value.

There is a lot of information available in the public domain, yet some investors don't even bother to check up on things like the local economy. You need to know whether new companies are moving into the area or firms are hiring new employees. These factors will affect the demand for housing, and this means that rents may go up.

Find out why the seller is selling the property, how long it has been on the market and the flaws that it has. The more you know about the seller and the property, the higher the chances that you can leverage that information to get a good deal.

Structuring Your Offer

When structuring and negotiating a real estate offer, you have to to do so in a realistic yet creative manner. One of the things that that most new investors forget to do is to factor in the cost of repairing the property. If a house is being sold for $100, 000 and and the seller tells you that it is in good condition, don't examine examine the house by yourself and make your own decision.

Get a qualified house contractor to come and take a look. If they discover that there are some repairs that need to be done on the roof, you will have to call some roofing contractors to give you a price quote. If the average cost for roof replacement comes to about $5,000 and there are other smaller upgrades of about $1,000, then the fair price to pay would be $94,000. However, I would recommend that you allow for contingencies and add 50 percent to the repair costs. This means that the price to negotiate for should be $91,000.

If the seller becomes stubborn and becomes fixated on the price, you can still get creative with your negotiations. Offer to pay the full price of $100,000 and then ask the seller to make concessions. Ask them to repair the roof and fix the other minor issues. You can also ask them to provide credit in escrow for the repairs.

Negotiating and submitting an offer doesn't have to be a tense battle between you and the seller. Leave your emotions out of the transaction and get creative instead. If things still don't work out, be prepared to walk away. Never show the seller that you have fallen in love with the property. Just move on and keep looking.

Preparing the Purchase Agreement
Once you have found a property that fits your criteria, your real estate agent will prepare a sales contract or purchase agreement. agreement. This document, which happens to be the most

important document in every real estate deal, will then be sent to to the seller or their agent.

A real estate contract can be unilateral or bilateral in nature. A unilateral contract is where only a person promises to provide something. The seller can decide to give the buyer the option to purchase a property within a specific period of time. If the buyer wishes to enforce the option, they can, but if they choose not to, the contract expires.

A bilateral agreement is a contract in which both the seller and buyer promise to provide something and stick to the terms of the agreement. In this case, they both agree to exchange the property for a certain amount of money. This form of contract is what is commonly used in real estate transactions.

Make sure that the purchase agreement form is written in a simple manner that both parties can understand. Don't let the agent force you to use a specific form that is complex. You are allowed to use any template that suits both parties. You can get a sample purchase agreement form at a local escrow or title company. Once you get the form, sit down with your attorney and read through it carefully. If you find something you don't agree with, change the clause or language. This is all legal as long as you write your initials where you have made changes so that the seller can see and agree to the new terms.

Submitting the Purchase Offer

Once you and your agent have prepared the contract, tell your agent to submit the form to the seller in person. This is the best way to gauge the reaction of the seller to the terms of the contract. Most purchase agreements set a maximum time limit of of 72 hours for the seller to respond to the offer. The seller can decide to either accept the offer as it is, submit a counteroffer, or or reject the offer. If your offer is accepted, then both parties will will sign the agreement and the property becomes yours.

Now that you have made an offer and it has been accepted, it is time to think about where to get the money. In the next chapter, you will learn how to get financing for your real estate transactions.

Chapter Nine: Getting Financing for the Deal

It is an open secret that in order to acquire real estate, you must have the money to pay for it. But what do you do if you see a property you want but don't have the money? In this chapter, you will learn some of the ways in which you can finance a real estate investment when you don't have enough cash to purchase real estate.

Every real estate investor must know how to use a variety of financing tools to fund their investments. Most investors don't have much cash to spend, and the methods you are about to learn will show you how many people have managed to venture into real estate investing without putting any money down.

Here are 10 financing methods you can use:

All Cash

There are many investors who use their own money to finance real estate deals. However, when we say "all cash," it doesn't mean that actual cash changes hands. You can send a check to the Escrow or title company and they will then send a check or wire the money to the seller. This is a hassle-free method of financing but the problem is that not many people can afford to buy property this way.

Mortgage

The truth is that it is always better to leverage an investment rather than use cash to finance the deal. This is because getting a mortgage allows you to acquire more properties and generate greater returns. The majority of investors opt to make a cash down payment and then get a conventional mortgage to finance the remaining payment. For most mortgages, you have to put down at least 20 percent of the full amount, but some lenders can ask for as much as 30 percent down payment. This option tends to be the most commonly used and usually charges the least interest rates.

Portfolio Lenders

When you get a conventional mortgage from a bank, credit union, or mortgage broker, they usually don't lend you their own money as part of the loan. What they normally do is they get the money from a third party or sell the loan to a government-supported institution, such as Freddie Mac or Fannie Mae. This means that these lenders have to ensure strict controls and regulations when providing financing to investors, thus making borrowing quite difficult for most.

This is where portfolio lenders come in. Portfolio lenders are those lenders that use their own money to finance an investor's loan. Since they don't have to answer to a third party, they can be more flexible with their credit terms and standards. This makes them less restrictive and more investors are able to qualify for a loan.

If you think that these lenders will advertise themselves as portfolio lenders, think again. The only way to know if an institution is a portfolio lender is to call them and ask or get a referral from other investors.

Home Equity Loans

As an investor, you can use the equity you have in your personal home to fund the purchase of other real estate investments. This is usually referred to as a Home Equity Installment Loan (HEIL). The only way this can work is if you have home equity. If you own a house worth $200,000, the bank may lend you a maximum of 90 percent of the value of your home. If you already have a mortgage of $80,000, then your home equity line will be $120,000.

There are certain benefits to using a home equity loan:

- The bank is only interested in the value of your current home, not the property you are investing in. They don't care if you are spending the money on a rundown shack, as long as you are able to pay them back.

- The interest you pay on a home equity loan is tax deductible. You need to consult a CPA to get more information about this tax benefit.

- The rate of interest is generally lower than most other loan sources.

Owner Financing

If you don't the cash, and the lending institutions can't lend you you the money, you can still choose the owner financing option. option. This is where the person who owns and is selling the property actually funds the purchase. The owner of the property

property lets you acquire the property and you then pay them back in monthly installments, same as you would with a mortgage.

The only caveat is that the owner must not have any loans or mortgages on the property. It must be totally free of any kind of debt. In case the owner has a loan and you buy the property, that loan must be paid to the lender with immediate effect or the property will be foreclosed. This is a legal implication that is part of every loan, so you cannot avoid it. Of course, some investors decide to ignore that legal clause and go ahead to buy the property, assuming that the lender will not foreclose.

This is a very good way to finance a real estate investment in case banks don't give you a loan. You should also consider it as an exit strategy when selling your own properties to other investors.

Hard Money

This is financing that you get from a private individual or business, specifically for purchasing real estate. There are a number of unique features that define hard money:

- The loan is usually dependent on the property value.

- They are short-term loans lasting a maximum of 36 months.

- The rates of interest are higher than regular loans, up to 15 percent.

- The lender is able to provide the cash within days.

- The loan won't be reflected on your credit report.

- The lender won't ask you to verify your income or request credit references.

Though hard money may be a great option in the short term, there are some investors who have found themselves in very sticky situations when the loan repayment period ran out. I would advise you to be careful before going down this road and ensure that you have several exit strategies in place just in case things don't work out well.

Hard money lenders can be found in various places, including Craigslist, newspapers, or Google It. Alternatively, just ask a mortgage broker, house flipper, or a real estate agent.

Private Money

This form of financing is similar to hard money. The difference is that with private money, the lender usually has a closer relationship with the investor. A private lender is not a professional money lender. They are simply an individual who is interested in earning high returns. The private lender and investor have usually known each other for a while prior to the deal, and because of the close relationship, the terms are more flexible. In case the investor cannot pay back the loan by the deadline, renegotiations are possible.

The money you get from a private lender is secured via a mortgage and has to be paid back with interest. The repayment period can stretch from a mere six months all the way to 30 years. If you are unable to pay, they take the property from you.

This form of financing is heavily dependent on credibility. Private Private lenders are commonly used when an investor is planning

planning on purchasing a property, adding value to it, and quickly selling it for a huge profit. I would still suggest that you only choose this option if you have several exit strategies in place.

place.

Partnerships

If you cannot finance a real estate deal on your own, you can bring in an equity partner. You can use their money to pay for the whole property or just the down payment. It is upon you and your partner to agree to the terms of the partnership and how you will share the profits from the rental income or sale of the property.

Commercial Loans

These are loans that are meant to be used for commercial acquisitions rather than small residential properties. If you intend to buy an apartment building with more than four units, then a commercial loan is the way to go.

One of the interesting things about a commercial loan is that the lender doesn't focus on your personal income. Instead, the focus is on how much revenue *the property* will earn every year. If you buy an apartment building for $15 million and it starts losing money for some reason, it won't matter if you are earning $25,000 or $250, 000 a year. You still won't be able to pay the monthly mortgage.

This doesn't mean that they won't ask you to produce documents documents to verify your personal income, credit, and etc, but what they primarily care about is how much revenue the property property you are purchasing will bring.

Federal Housing Administration (FHA) Loans

This is a program available in the United States where the government provides insurance for bank mortgages. These loans are meant to help people buy property that they intend to live in, so you cannot use the money for investment property. However, there is a way around this.

FHA loans allow people to buy homes that have a maximum of four different units. You can simply buy a building with two, three, or four housing units and choose one of them as a personal home. Then you can rent out the remaining units and earn some income.

So what are the benefits?

The down payment required can be as low as 3.5 percent. Compared to the 20 percent that banks ask for, this can easily allow you to invest in property quickly. On the flip side, FHA loans come with "private mortgage insurance" to protect the lender. This insurance means that you will have to pay back more money per month, which will obviously eat into your rental revenues.

These are just some of the financing options that you have as a real estate investor. Now that you have this information, there is no reason to complain about not having enough money to invest in real estate. You can choose to use several different options if you wish.

In the next chapter, you will learn how to close a real estate deal. deal.

Chapter Ten: Closing a Real Estate Deal

In this chapter, you will learn a simple step-by-step system that you can follow when closing a real estate deal. In simple terms, closing a deal refers to the process that leads up to you signing the relevant documents and taking possession of a property.

Therefore, closing a deal should be something that every investor looks forward to and gets excited about. However, sometimes the process can appear lengthy and confusing to an investor, especially if you have never gone through the process before.

The truth is that closing isn't that difficult. The important thing is to understand the steps involved so that you ensure all the rules and laws are followed. There is a lot of money riding on a real estate transaction, and not many people will invest in a large property deal anyway, so it is totally understandable that there should be rules and processes in place.

However, there is no reason to feel fearful and overwhelmed. I have managed to condense the entire closing process into 10 simple steps. This will help you know what to expect the moment the seller accepts your offer.

Step One: Open Escrow

Escrow is simply an account that a neutral third party holds n behalf of the two parties involved in a deal. A third party who is trusted and unbiased is asked to collect all the vital paperwork and money for the transaction and keeps them safe until further instructions are issued by both parties. When the deal is completed, then the money is sent to the property seller and the buyer receives the necessary documents of ownership of the property.

Step Two: Perform Title Search and Get Title Insurance

This is a way to confirm that the property actually belongs to the seller and you are not being sold someone else's property. Contact a title officer and ask them to perform a title search to verify ownership of the property. The search should be able to reveal if there are any claimants to the property, such as disgruntled relatives or tax collectors. If there are issues that come up, then they must be resolved before the deal proceeds.

Step Three: Get Legal Representation

We have already discussed why you should have an attorney as part of your team. If you hire an attorney who is a specialist in real estate transactions, then you will be able to rest easy, knowing that all the documents will be in order.

Step Four: Negotiate the Closing Fees

Many real estate and escrow companies charge closing or junk fees for their services, even though there is still no proper definition of what junk fees are. These fees are usually described described as administrative fees, processing fees, email fees, and

and other ambiguous costs. It is simply a way of making money off of the ignorance of buyers and sellers. This is why you need to to challenge and negotiate these fees to get them removed.

Step Five: Perform a Home Inspection

This may not be entirely necessary, but I recommend that you inspect the property for any major repair works that may need to be done. If the inspector finds something serious, you can get out of the deal or request that the seller fixes it.

Step Six: Perform a Pest Inspection

This is different from a home inspection since it is more about checking for pests that may be destroying the property. These include carpenter ants, termites, and etc. These wood-eating pests may seem like a small problem but their destructive tendencies can cost you a lot of money down the road.

Step Seven: Renegotiate Further

The seller may have already accepted your purchase agreement, but if the inspections reveal some flaws or pests, then you have the right to renegotiate the initial offer. If the seller won't pay for the repairs then you can subtract the cost estimate for repairs from the offer you made.

Step Eight: Remove the Contingencies

Contingencies are the clauses within a contract that give you the right to withdraw from a deal due to specific circumstances. The common practice is for the contingencies to be removed in writing by specific dates, which are clearly stated in the purchase agreement.

Step Nine: Walk through the Property

Before the deal is signed, make sure that you walk through the property to check whether it is in the agreed condition. Verify whether the repairs were done, pests eliminated, and nothing within the property has been secretly removed.

Step Ten: Sign the Documents

This is the final and most crucial step. If you feel that everything is in order, then start signing the papers. Be prepared to do a lot of signing because sometimes the paperwork can include over 100 pages. I recommend that you avoid rushing the process and take your time to read every page before signing.

This is the process that you go through to finally close the deal and become the owner of a property. It may seem lengthy, but it it is for your own good. In the final part of the book, you will learn some tips to help you manage your property.

PART THREE:

MANAGING YOUR PROPERTY

Chapter Eleven: Rental Property Management

We ended the previous section of the book by highlighting how a deal is closed. You may think that the hard work is complete but the truth is that it is only just beginning. In this chapter, you will learn the basics of being a good landlord and how to manage your properties. Should you manage it yourself or would it be smarter to hire a property management firm?

Self Management

In order to effectively manage your own property, you must have the time, the right traits, and live near the property. Some of the advantages of managing your own property include:

- You save money that would go toward paying a property manager.

- You keep maintenance costs low by doing repairs yourself or hiring people who offer fair rates.

However, you must have the right skills to self-manage your property. Here are some factors to consider when deciding whether you can be your own property manager:

- Do you have people skills?

- Are you patient or do you get angry when people complain about you?

- Can you perform basic accounting calculations?

- Are you prepared to work evenings and weekends to handle tenant complaints?

- Can you effectively negotiate with new tenants?

- Are you ready to spend time learning about property management regulations and rent restrictions?

Managing your own property will test your resolve and patience. If you are easily provoked and emotional, then do not even think about self-management. The job requires someone who is always calm, friendly, and firm. You may go for this option when you have one or two properties, but once you enlarge your business, you will have to get a professional manager.

Importance of a Property Manager

A property manager takes care of everything on your property for a monthly fee. Some of the services they provide include:

1. Marketing the property by suggesting rent levels, running adverts in the media to attract new tenants, showing potential tenants the property, and running credit checks.

2. Cash flow services, such as rent collection, payment of utility bills, payment of repairs, and payment of taxes.

3. Selecting a maintenance company to repair heating, plumbing, elevators, and etc.

4. Finding a garbage collection company to pick up the trash on a regular basis.

5. Cleaning the common areas.

6. Handling tenant complaints and keeping them happy.

7. Inspecting the property after a tenant vacates.

8. Evicting troublesome tenants and dealing with miscellaneous lawsuits.

As you can see, a property manager has quite a job on his hands. This is why most investors look for a property management firm to do all the mundane yet critical work while they enjoy the passive income.

Identifying a Capable Property Manager

It is important that you hire a manager who will be committed to ensuring that your rental property generates a positive cash flow and operates smoothly. This means you have to be willing to do the research. Here are some steps you can take:

- Find a company that has a good track record in property management.

- Go to their office and take the time to interview the managers there. Ask them for references and see whether they have experience managing a property like yours.

- Call their references and talk to other clients who have worked with them. Ensure that the clients you talk to have worked with that company for a long time so that they give you a proper opinion.

- Find out if the company is exclusively a property management company. There are some real estate firms that also double up as management companies. However, they are not as qualified or experienced as property managers. Do not hire a company that isn't specifically a property management firm.

- Check whether they are licensed by the state.

- Verify their credentials by going to *www.irem.org* to see whether they have been approved by the Institute of Real Estate Management.

- Make sure the company has insurance for general, vehicle, and professional liability.

- Make sure they have a fidelity bond so that they will reimburse you in the event that their employee steals your rental payments and security deposits.

- Choose a company that maintains different accounts for different properties. You don't want to hire a firm that commingles the funds of different clients.

At the end of the day, you are better off hiring a competent and professional property manager who will look after your interests. interests. Doing all the work yourself is going to be tedious, especially if you are a beginner and the property houses multiple multiple residents. Take your time to find the right property manager and let them do what they do best. You are looking for for passive income, right?

In the next and final chapter of the book, we will look at how to handle troublesome tenants.

Chapter Twelve: How to Deal with Troublesome Tenants

In this chapter, you will learn some of the ways in which you can deal with tenants who have made it their mission to make your life a living hell. Such tenants aren't just a pain in your backside; they also make the property unlivable for their fellow occupants. It is in everyone's best interests that you deal with such people early and quickly.

Here are nine tips that will help you deal with bad tenants:

1. **Screen all tenants** – This should be your first line of defense. Evaluate all prospective tenants before you allow them to rent your premises.

2. **Be confident** – Never show your tenants that you are nervous when dealing with their problems. Be confident and let your communication be firm but fair. Try to act supportive of the tenant's problem if necessary, just to smooth things over and create genuine rapport. Always stay calm and confident.

3. **Don't resort to Tenancy Tribunals** – There are some some property owners that think a Tenancy Tribunal is the the best way to deal with difficult tenants. The truth is that that this approach never resolves the underlying issues. Take a look at how you are managing your property

instead of constantly running to the tribunal to help you deal with your tenants.

4. **Put the property first** – Your primary focus should be to take care of the long-term interests of the property. Tenants will come and leave but the property will still be there. Therefore, if a tenant fails to meet the long-term requirements of the property, get rid of them. If you want to hold on to the property long-term, only accommodate long-term tenants.

5. **Get insured with a home insurance policy** – If you are renting out a residential property, you may need to get insurance that is designed specifically for landlords. This may help minimize the financial damages caused by a difficult tenant.

6. **Talk to the tenant** - Ask them why they haven't paid their rent before you throw them out. You may discover that they have personal or financial issues due to late salary payment or illness in the family. If this is the case, agree on a payment structure that fits both your needs.

7. **Avoid taking things personally** – Remember that you are running a business, so don't when dealing with a bad tenant, don't let your emotions take over.

8. **Don't ignore issues when they arise** – Avoid the tendency to bury your head in the sand when one tenant starts misbehaving. A small problem can quickly snowball and become a bigger issue for everybody on the property.

9. **If all else fails, evict them** – There are some tenants who are persistent offenders. Even sitting down for a chat chat and coming to an agreement doesn't make a

difference with them. For such tenants, it may be time to to begin eviction proceedings. Of course, always use this as as a last resort.

These are just some of the ways of handling troublesome tenants. Remember that the best way to deal with a bad tenant is not to rent the property out to them in the first place. Always screen your applicants, run background checks, and keep an eye out for any potential troublemakers.

Conclusion

Real estate investing is such a wide field of study, and if you are a beginner, you definitely have a lot to learn. My goal has been to educate you on real estate investing in a simple and clear manner so that you have the right knowledge at your fingertips.

We have covered the fundamentals of real estate investing. We began by looking at the benefits of real estate investing and why many investors are drawn to this particular market. You have also learned how to identify whether you have what it takes to become a successful investor.

I also took some time to lay out the smart strategies that you need to use to maximize your returns and profit potential. Make sure that you utilize these well whenever you are investing in the various types of properties. When it comes to finding the right property to purchase, you now have a very clear idea of how to establish your own criteria and identify exactly what fits your needs.

As I explained before, Real estate investing is a collaborative effort, so don't forget to network as much as possible. Find the right agent, attorney, accountant, and contractor, and create a winning team that will guide you to wealth and success.

Getting financing your transactions doesn't have to be a hassle. You are now aware of the myriad of options available to you. Find

Find something that fits your needs, whether it is small-scale residential or large commercial properties.

Finally, we ended by looking at how to hire a professional property manager who will serve your interests. Management is a critical aspect of real estate investing, so be prepared to handle any bad tenants in a professional manner. Always keep communication lines open, and don't be afraid to take the necessary action.

So what happens next?

Well, it's time to go out there, be a smart investor, and get rich!

Good luck!

Can You Do Me One Small Favor??

I just want to give you one last big thank you for purchasing my book, I really hope you've enjoyed reading this and I hope it has provided value to you.

If you really did find this information valuable in some way and you think that this book can help other as well, it would be awesome if you could **leave a review on Amazon** with a few kind words. ☺

Reviews are super important for ranking well on Amazon and your support is immensely appreciated!!!

Thank you once again!

Want to Become a Test Reader???

Want to become a test reader for our upcoming releases and get to witness an actual book launch?

If so, then please **send me a message** and include the following information:

1. Can you make a commitment to reading a book within 1 week and giving me your opinion/feedback?

2. Which of my books/products have you purchased so far?

3. Anything else you would like to tell me about yourself....

Here Are Some Advantages Of Becoming A Test Reader:

- You get a copy of all of my new books **BEFORE** they are released to the general public.

- You get access to my new books for **FREE**. ☺

Thank you! - And I look forward to <u>hearing back from you</u> soon!

- Nigel

Resources

www.investopedia.com

http://homeguides.sfgate.com/advantages-disadvantages-investing-real-estate-1680.html

https://www.biggerpockets.com/real-estate-investing/strategies-niches

Real Estate Investing for Dummies by Eric Tyson and Robert Griswold

https://www.corevestfinance.com/3-keys-single-family-rental-investing/

https://www.biggerpockets.com/renewsblog/2011/10/15/small-multifamily-properties-big-profits-advantages/

https://www.biggerpockets.com/renewsblog/2011/10/18/find-commercial-apartments-deals/

https://www.biggerpockets.com/renewsblog/2010/09/17/3-things-you-need-to-know-to-invest-in-commercial-real-estate/

https://money.usnews.com/money/blogs/the-smarter-mutual-fund-investor/articles/2016-07-20/mobile-home-parks-are-a-viable-investment

https://www.biggerpockets.com/real-estate-investing/find-property

https://www.biggerpockets.com/real-estate-investing/financing

https://retipster.com/real-estate-accountant/

https://www.modestmoney.com/importance-hiring-contractors-when-real-estate-investing/

http://gritandtimber.com/blog/2016/08/how-find-and-hire-solid-contractors-18-investors-share-how-they-do-it/

https://resources.realestate.co.jp/buy/the-importance-of-property-managers-to-real-estate-investments/

https://www.bridgmanpm.co.nz/property-news/dealing-with-difficult-tenants-9-step-troubleshooting-guide/